WELCOME TO MY COUNTRY

Welcome to
NIGERIA

Gareth Stevens Publishing
A WORLD ALMANAC EDUCATION GROUP COMPANY

Written by
ESTHER KERR/YINKA ISMAIL

Edited in USA by
DOROTHY L. GIBBS

Designed by
GEOSLYN LIM

Picture research by
SUSAN JANE MANUEL

First published in North America in 2002 by
Gareth Stevens Publishing
A World Almanac Education Group Company
330 West Olive Street, Suite 100
Milwaukee, Wisconsin 53212 USA

Please visit our web site at:
www.garethstevens.com
For a free color catalog describing
Gareth Stevens Publishing's list of high-quality
books and multimedia programs,
call 1-800-542-2595 or
fax your request to (414) 332-3567.

© **TIMES MEDIA PRIVATE LIMITED 2002**
Originated and designed by
Times Editions
an imprint of Times Media Private Limited
Times Centre, 1 New Industrial Road
Singapore 536196
http://www.timesone.com.sg/te

Library of Congress Cataloging-in-Publication Data
Kerr, Esther.
Welcome to Nigeria / Esther Kerr and Yinka Ismail.
p. cm. — (Welcome to my country)
Summary: Describes the history, geography, economy, government,
language and arts, and social life and customs of Nigeria.
Includes bibliographical references and index.
ISBN 0-8368-2537-3 (lib. bdg.)
1. Nigeria—Juvenile literature. [1. Nigeria.]
I. Ismail, Yinka. II. Title. III. Series.
DT515.58.K47   2002
966.9—dc21   2002022389

Printed in Malaysia

1 2 3 4 5 6 7 8 9 06 05 04 03 02

PICTURE CREDITS
Archive Photos: 27, 36 (top)
Art Directors and Trip Photo Library: 1,
  3 (top), 7 (bottom), 9, 21, 22, 30, 37
Camera Press: 14, 29 (both), 33 (top),
  36 (bottom)
Camerapix: cover, 2, 16, 19, 20 (top),
  41 (bottom)
Victor Englebert: 5, 28
Hulton Getty/Archive Photos: 13 (top left),
  13 (top right)
Hutchison Library: 3 (bottom), 4, 8, 11, 18,
  20 (bottom), 26, 38, 41 (top)
Björn Klingwall: 6, 7 (top), 17 (bottom), 25,
  31, 32, 34, 40, 43, 45
Jason Laure: 3 (center), 23, 24, 33 (bottom),
  35, 39
Nigerian High Commission of Singapore:
  44 (both)
North Wind Picture Archives: 10
Topham Picturepoint: 12, 13 (bottom),
  15 (top), 15 (bottom), 17 (top)

Digital Scanning by Superskill Graphics Pte Ltd

Contents

Words that appear in the glossary are printed in **boldface** type the first time they occur in the text.

Welcome to Nigeria!

The Federal Republic of Nigeria has the largest population in Africa. This country is sometimes called "the Giant of Africa" because it is home to more than 250 **ethnic groups**, as well as an extraordinary variety of animals and plants. Let's learn more about the rich cultures and friendly people of Nigeria.

Opposite: These Nigerian men are wearing traditional clothing to celebrate a religious festival.

Below: In Kano, the central mosque towers high above other buildings.

The Flag of Nigeria

Nigeria's flag is called the Nigerian National and Merchant Flag and Jack. Officially adopted in 1960, it has two green vertical bands with a white band between them. Green stands for the land; white stands for peace and unity.

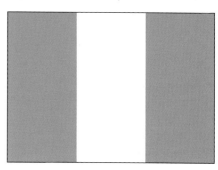

The Land

Nigeria is bigger than Texas. It covers 356,700 square miles (923,853 square kilometers) and is Africa's fourteenth largest country. To the north, it shares its border with Niger. Cameroon and Chad are to the east. Benin is to the west. The country's southern coastline is on the Gulf of Guinea and the South Atlantic Ocean.

Nigeria was named after the Niger River, the third longest river in Africa. The Niger is 2,600 miles (4,183 km)

Below: Ferries are an important form of transportation on the Niger River.

long. It enters Nigeria in the northwest and empties into the Gulf of Guinea in the South Atlantic Ocean. The Niger is one of many rivers in Nigeria.

The country has four different types of **terrain**. In the south, the fan-shaped Niger **Delta** is mostly swampland. The area north of the delta is a tropical rain forest. Open grasslands called savannas are north of the rain forest. Far north, near the Sahara Desert, the land is dry and sandy. Chappal Waddi, in eastern Nigeria, is the highest mountain. It is 7,936 feet (2,419 meters) high.

Above: Many **nomadic** tribes live on the savanna around Lake Chad.

Below: Bananas are one of many kinds of fruits grown in Nigeria.

Climate

Located between the equator and the Tropic of Cancer, Nigeria has a climate that is hot all year long. Temperatures vary from region to region, depending on the amount of rainfall a region gets. The Jos Plateau, which is 4,200 feet (1,280 m) above sea level, has some of the lowest temperatures in the country. The semidesert region in the north is hot, with temperatures reaching up to 100° Fahrenheit (38° Celsius). For five months each year, Nigeria's climate is also affected by the harmattan wind.

Below:
Between November and March, the hot, dry harmattan wind blows across most of Nigeria from the Sahara Desert and covers the country with dust.

Plants and Animals

Hardwood trees, such as mahogany and teak, as well as rubber and cocoa trees, grow well in Nigeria's tropical rain forest. Acacia and **baobab** trees thrive in the drier areas between the savannas and the northern semidesert.

Nigeria's wildlife includes giraffes and lions on the grasslands, monkeys and elephants in the rain forest, and crocodiles in the rivers. The country also has more than 350 kinds of birds.

History

The Noks, who lived in Nigeria from about 500 B.C. to A.D. 200, are believed to be the country's first **civilization**. One of the most important kingdoms, however, was Kanem-Bornu, which ruled in northeastern Nigeria from the ninth to the nineteenth centuries. This empire gained great wealth by trading kola nuts and ivory at markets across the Sahara Desert.

Below:
The history of Kano state, in northern Nigeria, dates back to the tenth century. Trade in the Sahara brought wealth to the city of Kano.

Trading also brought Islam to the country. The Islamic Hausa empire had established several separate **city-states** in central and northwestern Nigeria by the tenth century. These city-states were rivals to each other, as well as to the neighboring Kanem-Bornu empire.

A third great empire, the Fulani, finally replaced both of these savanna kingdoms and brought them under one system of government. Fulani nomads led by Usman dan Fodio (1754–1817) defeated the Hausa city-states by 1808. Kanem-Bornu fell in 1846.

In southwestern Nigeria, Yoruba kingdoms ruled from the eleventh to the sixteenth centuries. In the 1200s, the Edo people founded the kingdom of Benin, which controlled a large area northwest of the Niger Delta. The Edo traded slaves to Europeans for cloth and other goods. Because of the slave trade, this part of the African coast was called the "Slave Coast."

Above:
The ancient Benin empire is known for its bronze and **terracotta** sculptures.

The First Europeans

The Portuguese were the first Europeans in Nigeria. Searching for trade routes, Prince Henry of Portugal (1394–1460) sent expeditions to the western coast of Africa. The Portuguese landed at Benin in 1472. At first, they traded for ivory, gold, and pepper. Later, they traded for slaves. By the late seventeenth century, the British were the biggest European slave traders in Nigeria.

Below:
The British set up trading posts, like this one in Asaba, along the Niger River in southern Nigeria.

Trade and Christianity

The British ended their slave trade in 1807 because of public protests against it. Looking for new ways to trade with Africa, they explored the country. In 1823, a Scottish explorer named Hugh Clapperton (1788–1827) helped open up trade with northern Nigeria. Soon, Christian missionaries arrived. The Methodists established a mission post in 1843. The Roman Catholics set up their first church in 1885.

Above: Scotsmen Mungo Park (*right*) and Hugh Clapperton (*left*) both explored the Niger River.

Below: Flora Shaw, a British journalist, suggested naming Nigeria after the Niger River.

Colonization and Independence

Realizing how important trade was on the Niger River, the Europeans divided western Africa among themselves. The British controlled Nigeria. In 1914, it was called the Colony and Protectorate of Nigeria. On October 1, 1960, Britain granted Nigeria independence. In 1966, however, the Nigerian army took over the government. Nigeria's **democracy** was restored when Olusegun Obasanjo was elected president in May 1999.

Below:
These Nigerians are celebrating Independence Day on a colorfully decorated float.

Amina Sarauniya Zazzua (c. 1533–c. 1610)

Although she was not the queen of Zazzua until 1576, Amina Sarauniya started learning how to rule at the age of sixteen. During her reign, Zazzua grew to be a powerful city-state.

Frederick John Lugard (1858–1945)

India-born Frederick John Lugard was the British soldier put in charge of establishing control over Nigeria in the 1890s. In 1914, Lugard was appointed Nigeria's first governor general. He retired in 1919.

Frederick John Lugard

Nnamdi Azikiwe (1904–1996)

Known as the father of Nigeria's independence, Nnamdi Azikiwe was Nigeria's first president (1963 to 1966). He also founded a political party called the National Council of Nigeria and the Cameroon.

Nnamdi Azikiwe

Government and the Economy

Nigeria is divided into thirty-six states and the capital territory of Abuja, and it has three levels of government. The president, vice president, and a cabinet head the federal government. Each of the states has a governor and a House of Assembly. Local governments are run by elected councils. State and local governments take care of issues such as health, education, and transportation.

Left:
Nigeria's Parliament House is in the new capital, Abuja. Lagos was Nigeria's capital until December 1991.

Left:
Inspectors are sent by the government to check the quality of Nigeria's peanuts. Most of the peanuts are exported.

Laws are passed by the National Assembly, which has a Senate and a House of Representatives elected by the people. The country's courts follow English common law, Islamic law, and tribal law.

Below: Palm oil, one of Nigeria's main agricultural exports, comes from the reddish orange fruit of the oil palm tree.

Agriculture

Nigeria's main agricultural products are cocoa and palm oil from the rain forest in the south and peanuts grown on the savannas in the north.

Exports and Trade

Oil is Nigeria's most important natural resource. Nigeria is Africa's biggest oil producer and the world's sixth biggest oil exporter. It supplies oil to both the United States and Britain. Other major exports include cocoa, rubber, and tin. Nigeria's main trading partners are the United States and the European Union. Its main imports include machinery and building materials.

Above:
These workers are operating machinery on an oil rig. Oil was discovered in Nigeria in 1956.

The Workforce

Many Nigerians are unemployed or work in unskilled jobs, such as parking or cleaning cars. More than half of the workforce is involved in agriculture. Most of the rest have service jobs.

Transportation

Nigeria has a wide network of roads and railways, but they are in very poor condition. Three major ocean ports and three international airports link Nigeria with the rest of the world.

Below: Traffic jams are more and more common in Lagos and other large cities as Nigerians continue to move away from country towns and villages.

People and Lifestyle

With more than 126 million people, Nigeria is the most heavily populated country in Africa. More than two-thirds of the country's people belong to three main ethnic groups, the Hausa-Fulani, the Yoruba, and the Igbo, or Ibo.

About 43 percent of Nigerians live in cities, where they may have modern conveniences, such as electricity and indoor plumbing, but where poverty,

Above: This girl is a member of the Hausa-Fulani group. The Hausa-Fulani are cattle herders who live in northern and central Nigeria.

Left: In northern Nigeria, young Wodaabe men dress up and put on makeup to compete in a traditional male beauty contest.

overcrowding, and crime are major problems. In spite of these problems, Nigerians are friendly and have a great sense of humor.

Families

Nigerians have large families, and family ties, even with aunts, uncles, and cousins, are extremely important. Especially among the Yoruba, respect for older adults is also very important.

Women in Nigeria

Women play active roles in Nigerian communities. Many of them have jobs in business or academic fields or hold positions of leadership in government or international organizations, such as the International Monetary Fund or the World Bank. Even Muslim women, who must stay in their homes, can earn an income spinning cotton or cooking bean cakes and millet dumplings.

National Service

All college and university graduates must complete military training and job service in the Nigerian National Youth Service Corps. Some complete their national service duties by teaching.

Nigerian Names

Names are important to Nigerians. A baby is named in a ceremony held one week after its birth. Names are usually religious and a short form of a sentence.

Below: After their national service, some Nigerian men join the country's armed forces.

Education

Nigerian parents value education, and, today, most Nigerian children attend school. Only about half of Nigerian people over age fifteen are **literate**, yet the country has produced experts in many fields of learning.

Children in Nigeria start elementary school at age six. Along with subjects such as mathematics and science, they study English and Nigeria's three main

Below:
These students are learning to play the recorder. Some of Nigeria's private schools offer music classes.

languages — Hausa, Yoruba, and Igbo. After six years of elementary school, they must pass the Common Entrance Examination to go on to secondary school, or high school. In six years of high school, students must pass three more important examinations.

Nigeria strongly encourages higher education, and the country has sixty-three universities and **polytechnic** colleges for students to choose from.

Religion

Islam and Christianity are the main religions in Nigeria. Traders crossing the Sahara Desert brought Islam into the country in the eleventh century. Catholic Portuguese traders brought Christianity to Nigeria in the 1400s. Today, about 50 percent of Nigerians are Muslims, and about 40 percent are Christians. The remaining 10 percent practice traditional African religions.

Above:
These Muslims have gathered for prayers at a mosque in Kano. Most of Nigeria's Muslims live in the country's northern cities and villages.

Most traditional African religions are based on animism, which is the belief that all natural objects have a spirit. Many of these religions also practice ancestor worship and offer animal **sacrifices** to please gods and other spirits. Some of the traditional African religions include Christian or Muslim beliefs. The Aladura (ah-lah-DOO-rah) Church, for example, is a combination of the traditional Yoruba religion and Christianity.

Below: Christians sing at a church service in Lagos. Christianity is the main religion in southern Nigeria.

Language

Nigeria has over 250 languages and **dialects**, but English is the country's official language. Many Nigerians speak pidgin English, a mixture of standard and mispronounced English words, slang, and words from native languages. Hausa, Igbo, and Yoruba are Nigeria's main native languages.

Left: A young Hausa man carefully copies pages of the Qur'an in Arabic script.

Literature

Traditionally, the history and culture of Nigeria is handed down orally in stories, songs, and sayings, but Nigeria also has some very gifted writers. Wole Soyinka (1934–), a Nigerian who has Yoruba roots, has written two novels, four volumes of poetry, and more than twenty plays. Igbo schoolteacher Flora Nwapa (1931–) was the first Nigerian woman to publish a novel in English.

Above: Ben Okri (1959–) (*left*) and Wole Soyinka (*right*) are award-winning Nigerian writers.

Arts

The history of Nigerian art dates back over 2,000 years. Nok sculptures made of terra-cotta are the earliest known art forms. Archaeologists have also found beautiful bronze, terra-cotta, and wood sculptures of both human and mythical figures from the ancient kingdom of Benin. Nigerian art celebrates life and reflects the cultures and traditions of the country's many ethnic groups.

Below: These figures were carved into the walls of Benin City centuries ago.

Modern Art

Jimoh Buraimoh, Bruce Onobrakpeya, and Musa Yola are modern Nigerian artists. Buraimoh was famous in the 1960s for his beautiful **mosaics** made of thousands of glass beads glued to wood. Onobrakpeya is known for his molded plastic figures. Yola paints the fronts of houses and other buildings with flowers, checkerboard patterns, and human figures.

Above: This Igbo craftsman is making an animal sculpture out of wood.

Decorative Arts

In some Nigerian communities, artists work together in small groups, making crafts such as weaving, basketry, and pottery. They also use their skills to decorate useful items, such as bowls. Decorating calabash gourds is a special Nigerian art. The fruit is scooped out of the gourd, and designs are carved into its outer skin. Decorated gourds are often used as storage containers.

Music and Dance

Music has always been important in Nigerian culture. Traditional Nigerian music includes *agidigbo* (ah-GEE-DIG-boh), *kokoma* (koh-koh-MAH), and *juju* (JOO-joo).

Dancing in Nigeria is important in religious **rituals** and special events, as well as for entertainment. The lively, colorful Nigerian dances are performed to the beat of African drums. At Igbo festivals, dancers sometimes perform wearing colorfully painted masks.

Above: Famous Nigerian singer Fela Kuti introduced a new style of music in the 1970s. Called Afro-beat, this new style blended the rhythms of Africa with the soul music of America.

Left: Traditional Hausa dances are popular at outdoor concerts in Lagos.

33

Leisure

Nigerians like to entertain friends at home, watching television and videos and listening to music. Watching TV is a particularly popular pastime, and Nigeria offers TV viewers about forty television channels.

Games are another favorite activity. Nigerians play checkers and chess, as well as traditional African games. *Ayo*

Below: Nigerians like to shop and meet friends at the country's crowded roadside markets.

(AH-yo) is an ancient game Yorubas play using seeds on a carved wooden board. Igbos call this game *okwe* (OH-kway). Hausas call it *darra* (DAH-rah).

Above: Most towns in Nigeria have a sports field or a stadium for soccer games and track and field events.

Sports

Nigerians enjoy many sports, including basketball, volleyball, and rugby, but soccer is the country's national sport. Wealthy Nigerians play tennis and golf, and almost everyone plays Ping-Pong.

International Sports Stars

Some Nigerian athletes, especially in soccer, track and field, and boxing, are international stars. Celestine Babayaro plays for Chelsea, one of the United Kingdom's top soccer clubs. Nigeria's national soccer team, the Super Eagles, won an Olympic gold medal in 1996. At the 2000 Olympics, Nigerians won silver medals in women's weightlifting, **hurdling**, and the men's 1600-meter relay. Toronto Raptors basketball star Hakeem Olajuwon was born in Lagos.

Above: Nigerian Nwankwo Kanu plays soccer for the United Kingdom's Arsenal Football Club.

Religious Holidays

Muslims throughout Nigeria celebrate *Id al-Fitr* (EED ahl-FIT-reh) at the end of **Ramadan**. The most colorful celebrations are in northern Nigeria, where the festivities include the *sallah* (SAH-lah) ceremony. Hausa-Fulani horsemen, dressed in armor, charge on decorated horses toward the emir, or traditional leader. They stop abruptly at the emir's throne and salute him.

Below: A cavalry procession is part of the Id al-Fitr celebration in the city of Kano.

River Festivals

A three-day fishing festival held each February in Argungu brings visitors to Nigeria from all over the world. During this festival, hundreds of people jump into the Sokoto River and try to catch the biggest fish.

The Pategi Regatta is held in August on the Niger River. Boat racing is the main event, but fishing, swimming, and **acrobatics** are also part of the festival.

Below: At the Argungu Fishing Festival, people use nets, calabash gourds, and even their bare hands to catch fish.

Other Festivals

National Day in Nigeria is held on October 1, celebrating the day the country won its independence from Britain, in 1960. Military parades are part of the festivities.

Some Igbo clans celebrate *Ikeji* (ee-KAY-jee), which is a music and dance festival. *Igue* (ee-GOO-ay) is a cultural festival in Benin City that celebrates the start of a new year.

Above: Colorful, inflated "bouncy castles" are part of the fun at this children's festival in Lagos.

Food

Corn, rice, beans, yams, millet, and **tapioca** are common foods in Nigeria. All of these foods can be pounded into flour, mixed with water, and cooked as a paste. Pastes are rolled into little balls and eaten with thick soups. A favorite soup, made with meat or fish, onions, red peppers, crushed melon seeds, and spinach, is called *egusi* (ee-GOO-see).

Below: Family members prepare traditional Nigerian meals together.

Nigerian cooking often includes chili peppers, herbs, and spices such as garlic, ginger, and cloves. Many dishes also include rice. *Jollof* (JAW-lof) is a well-known Nigerian dish. It is rice cooked with tomatoes and meat. Fried rice and coconut rice are popular, too.

Beans are a favorite snack food. Black-eyed beans are often eaten plain, but they are also made into cake called *moyin-moyin* (MOH-yeen-MOH-yeen). *Akara* (ah-KAH-rah) is a fried bean snack. A snack called *kulikuli* (KOO-lee-KOO-lee) is a ball of peanut paste.

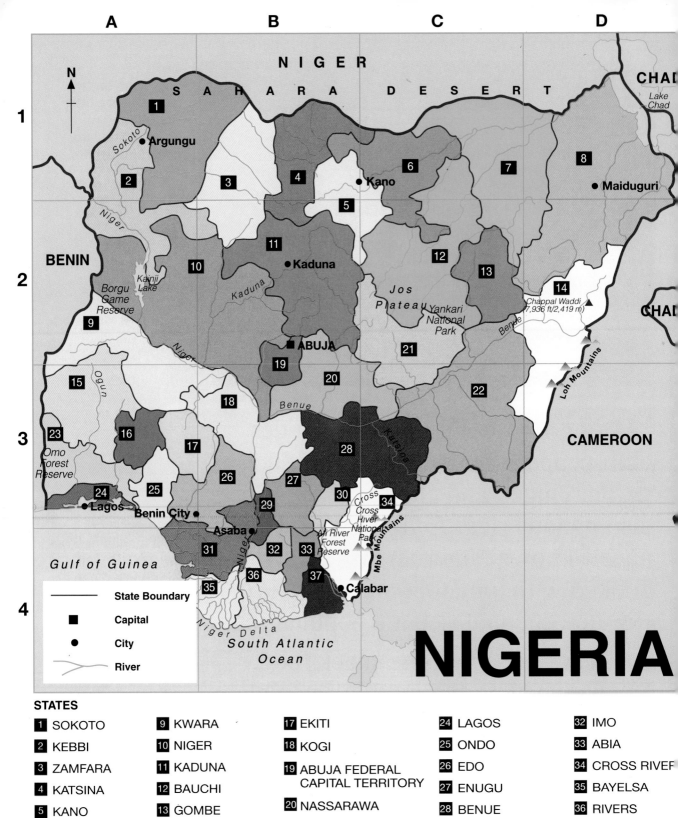

NIGERIA

STATES

1 SOKOTO	**9** KWARA	**17** EKITI	**24** LAGOS	**32** IMO
2 KEBBI	**10** NIGER	**18** KOGI	**25** ONDO	**33** ABIA
3 ZAMFARA	**11** KADUNA	**19** ABUJA FEDERAL CAPITAL TERRITORY	**26** EDO	**34** CROSS RIVER
4 KATSINA	**12** BAUCHI		**27** ENUGU	**35** BAYELSA
5 KANO	**13** GOMBE	**20** NASSARAWA	**28** BENUE	**36** RIVERS
6 JIGAWA	**14** ADAMAWA	**21** PLATEAU	**29** ANAMBRA	**37** AKWA IBOM
7 YOBE	**15** OYO	**22** TARABA	**30** EBONYI	
8 BORNO	**16** OSUN	**23** OGUN	**31** DELTA	

Above: Lagos is a large, modern city on the Gulf of Guinea.

Abuja B2
Alf River Forest
    Reserve B4
Argungu A1
Asaba B4

Benin A1–A3
Benin City A3
Benue River B3–D2
Borgu Game
    Reserve A2

Calabar B4
Cameroon D1–C4
Chad D1 and D2
Chappal Waddi D2
Cross River B4–C3
Cross River
    National Park
    B3–C4

Gulf of Guinea
    A3–A4

Jos Plateau C2

Kaduna B2
Kaduna River B2
Kainji Lake A2
Kano B1
Katsina River C3

Lagos A3
Lake Chad D1
Loh Mountains
    D2–D3

Maiduguri D1
Mbe Mountains
    B4–C3

Niger A1–D1
Niger Delta B4
Niger River A2–B4

Ogun River A3
Omo Forest
    Reserve A3

Sahara Desert
    A1–D1
Sokoto River A1–B1
South Atlantic
    Ocean A4–C4

Yankari National
    Park C2

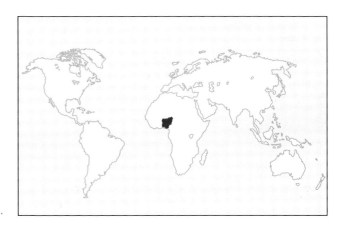

Quick Facts

Official Name	Federal Republic of Nigeria
Capital	Abuja
Official Language	English
Native Languages	Hausa, Yoruba, Igbo, Fulfulde
Population	126.6 million (2001 estimate)
Land Area	356,700 square miles (923,853 square km)
Highest Point	Chappal Waddi 7,936 feet (2,419 m)
Major Rivers	Benue, Kaduna, Niger, Sokoto
Major Lakes	Chad, Kainji
Major Cities	Abuja, Kano, Lagos
Main Religions	Islam, Christianity
Major Imports	Building materials, food products, live animals, machinery, manufactured goods, transportation equipment
Major Exports	Cocoa, oil and petroleum products, rubber
Major Festivals	National Day (October 1) Id al-Fitr
Currency	Nigerian Naira (NGN 123 = U.S. $1 in 2002)

Opposite: *Masquerade* is one of Nigerian artist Jimoh Buraimoh's glass bead mosaics.

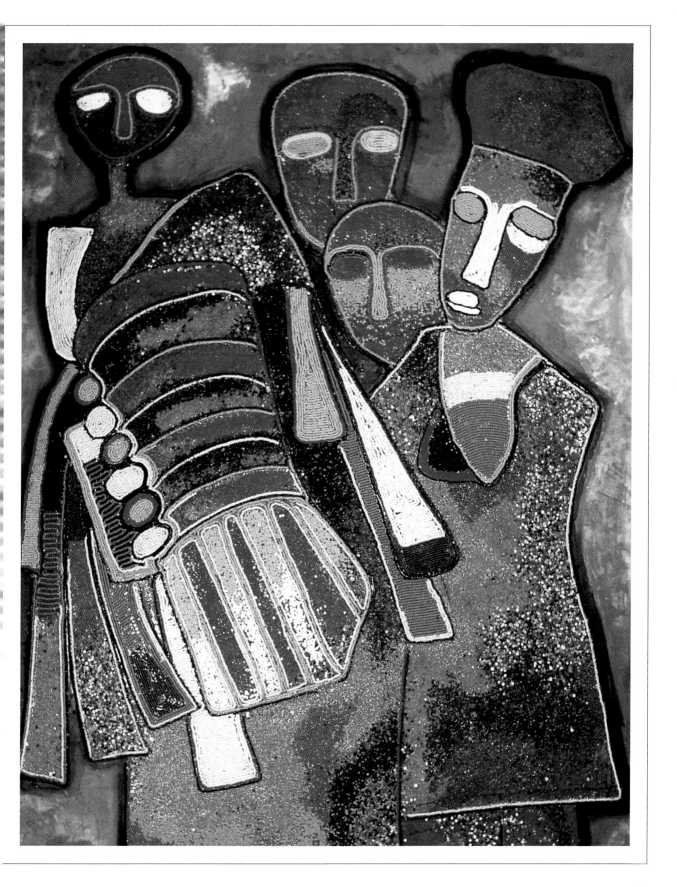

45

Glossary

acrobatics: displays of physical skills that require great strength, flexibility, and body control, such as tumbling or walking a tightrope.

baobab: a large tree found in tropical Africa, which has a very thick trunk and fruit that looks like gourds.

cavalry: an army of soldiers who fight on horseback.

city-states: single cities that have the political power of a nation, such as ancient Rome and Athens.

civilization: a society that has a highly developed culture and government and an established, written record of its history.

delta: a flat, triangle-shaped area of land, formed by deposits of sand and soil at the mouth of a river.

democracy: a political system in which people rule themselves by electing representatives to make laws and run the government.

dialects: forms of a particular language that are spoken only in certain places or by certain groups of people.

ethnic groups: large groups of people who share a common race, culture, language, religion, or way of life.

hurdling: a track and field event performed by runners who must jump over frames or fences in the course of a race.

literate: able to read and write.

mosaics: works of art made by setting small pieces of colored stone, tile, or glass into glue or cement to form a picture or a design.

nomadic: related to groups of people who have no permanent home and move together from place to place.

polytechnic: related to the teaching of technical skills and applied sciences.

Ramadan: the month in the Islamic calendar when Muslims do not eat anything between sunrise and sunset.

rituals: particular words or actions that are always said or done the same way, usually as part of a ceremony.

sacrifices: acts of offering or giving up something to God as a sign of faith and devotion.

tapioca: a starchy food that comes from the root of a tropical plant and is often mixed into liquid foods to make them thicker.

terra-cotta: hard, baked, reddish brown clay that has no glaze, or coating.

terrain: the main features that describe the landscape of a geographic area.

More Books to Read

The Benin Kingdom of West Africa.
    John Peffer-Engels
    (Powerkids Press)

*The Magic Tree: A Folktale from
    Nigeria.* T. Obinkaram Echewa
    (Morrow Junior)

Metropolis: An Ancient African Town.
    Fiona MacDonald (Franklin Watts)

Nigeria. Countries of the World series.
    Kristin Thoennes (Capstone Press)

Nigeria. Festivals of the World series.
    Elizabeth Berg (Gareth Stevens)

Nigeria. We Come from series. Alison
    Brownlie (Raintree Steck-Vaughn)

*Nigeria: The Land. Lands, People,
    and Cultures* series. Bobbie
    Kalman (Crabtree)

Nigeria: One Nation, Many Cultures.
    Hassan Adeeb (Benchmark Books)

*Ogbo: Sharing Life in an African
    Village.* Ifeoma Onyefulu
    (Gulliver Books)

*A Triangle for Adaora. An African Book
    of Shapes.* Ifeoma Onyefulu
    (Dutton Books)*

Videos

*Africa: A History Denied. Lost
    Civilizations* series. (Time-Life)

Africa: The Story of a Continent.
    (Home Vision Entertainment)

Worlds Together: West Africa.
    (Library Video)

*Yoruba: Nine Centuries of African Art
    and Culture.* (Insight Media)

Web Sites

www.folklife.si.edu/vfest/africa/
    start.htm

www.hamillgallery.com/NOK/
    NokTerracottas/Nok.html

www.motherlandnigeria.com/
    kidzone.html

www.nigeriaembassyusa.org/
    thisisnigeria.shtml

Due to the dynamic nature of the Internet, some web sites stay current longer than
others. To find additional web sites, use a reliable search engine with one or more
of the following keywords to help you locate information about Nigeria. Keywords:
Argungu, Benin, Igbo, jollof, Lagos, Niger River, Nok, Yankari National Park.

Index